The Georgia Open History Library has been made possible in part by a major grant from the National Endowment for the Humanities: Democracy demands wisdom. Any views, findings, conclusions, or recommendations expressed in this collection, do not necessarily represent those of the National Endowment for the Humanities.

NATIONAL
ENDOWMENT
FOR THE
HUMANITIES

COVER PAGE OF THE LAWS

Laws of the Creek Nation

Edited by
ANTONIO J. WARING

UNIVERSITY OF GEORGIA LIBRARIES
MISCELLANEA PUBLICATIONS, NO. 1

UNIVERSITY OF GEORGIA PRESS
ATHENS   1960

Reissue published in 2021

Most University Press titles are available
from popular e-book vendors.

Printed digitally

ISBN 9780820360997 (Hardcover)
ISBN 9780820360980 (Paperback)
ISBN 9780820360973 (Ebook)

Copyright © 1960 by UNIVERSITY OF GEORGIA PRESS
Library of Congress Catalog Card Number: 60-9142

Printed in the United States of America

Contents

Foreword to the Reissue	vii
Foreword *by* W. P. Kellam	xiii
INTRODUCTION	1
LAWS OF THE CREEK NATION	17

Foreword to the Reissue

On July 9, 2020, the U.S. Supreme Court issued a landmark ruling in *McGirt v. Oklahoma*, recognizing that the Muscogee (Creek) Nation's promised reservation, as established by treaty in 1866 in Indian Territory, still has legal status as a reservation in the twenty-first century. Once again, the people of the Muscogee (Creek) Nation (MCN), known as the Mvskokvlke, have persevered despite the odds.

As the contemporary MCN prepares to retake the reins of self-government within the boundaries of the reservation, it is perhaps an ideal time in which to reflect on the legal history of the Mvskokvlke people. As one of the first tribal nations in the United States to codify its laws in English, the legal story of the Mvskokvlke also offers insight into the development of tribal statutory development in the nineteenth century. It also offers glimpses of Mvskoke legal principles and values that predate the establishment of the United States.

Waring's original 1960 introduction contains a full treatment of the historical context in which these laws were communicated to the Georgia governor and offers insight into the sum of the laws themselves. As we approach the two hundredth anniversary of the Treaty of Indian Springs, it is worth considering how these laws continue to have relevance for contemporary Mvskokvlke and for the fields of American Indian studies and Indian law. This twenty-first-century reflection provides some insight into what contemporary readers of the document can learn about Mvskoke laws and culture, with a fresh perspective on some of the important gendered and racialized laws.

These 1824 McIntosh laws were not the first written laws of the Mvskoke people. In 1818, a list of eleven written laws (primarily criminal) was presented to David Brydie Mitchell, the Indian agent to the Creek Nation, signed by Chilly McIntosh's father, William, and four other Creek leaders. The 1824 laws expanded on the 1818 laws, with many of the same laws appearing in the 1824 version, which had over fifty-five laws.

We know that Chilly McIntosh, who served as the clerk to the Creek National Council and as an interpreter for the council's laws, hand-scribed the laws passed by the Creek National Council between 1817 and 1824. At that time, there was no written Mvskoke language—that would come several years later, after removal to Indian Territory, when Christian missionaries needed a written language to teach and spread the gospel. By the late 1840s and early 1850s, Creek leaders and Christian missionaries formalized a written Mvskoke language that continues to this day.[1]

We do not know the precise method by which the McIntosh laws were passed or recorded. Typically, the Grand Council in this time period met at least once a year.[2] It's likely that the laws were passed in the Mvskoke language and Chilly McIntosh translated them into English for codification purposes. To the extent that there might be some concepts that could be lost in translation, it's important to note that Chilly McIntosh himself could be characterized as a highly assimilated Creek who was also a baptized Christian. This may have colored both his intentions and translations.

The laws themselves offer a fascinating glimpse into the working of Mvskoke law and governance. Of the fifty-seven laws, at least twenty can be characterized as criminal in nature, including several substantive laws prohibiting murder, rape, adultery, and theft. In addition, the laws reference criminal defenses, including self-defense and intoxication. In terms of sanctions, the murder laws all provide for execution of the offender. Other crimes have an escalating series of sanctions for repeat offenders: for the first offense, the offender would be whipped; for the second offense, the offender would be cropped (ear cut off); and for the third offense, the offender would be executed.

Laws pertaining to governance and leadership offer a glimpse into some of the intragovernment struggles that the Mvskoke people were experiencing. The 28th law, dated as passed in 1819, acknowledges that there had been issues with town governments (independent local Mvskoke governments) seceding from the national government. Such seceding towns "shall have no claims upon this Country without the Consent of the Hole Nation." There had also apparently been issues with law enforcement officials failing to enforce the laws or using their position to abuse others. The second law, numbered as 32nd, requires the termination ("broke") of such law enforcement officials. Slander against government officials was prohibited by the 43rd law, which reads, "If person or persons should give bad talk against Warriors or chiefs, he shall be punish." Perhaps the most significant law in this category is the 33rd, which requires that persons who "tell such lies as should be brought to disturpence of the Nation" could be executed. Some historians believe that this may be the law that compelled the execution of Chilly's father, William McIntosh, for treason in 1825 for signing a removal treaty without authorization.

Also clear is that the Mvskokvlke people were struggling to maintain control over white men's behavior on their lands. Five of the laws (19th, 41st, 42nd, 49th, and 55th) specifically mention "White Man." It is clear that the drafters of these laws sought to exclude white men from their lands unless they had received formal governmental approval. The 49th law prohibits allowing a white man into the nation unless "the hole Nation agree to it." A white man who worked for a Mvskoke citizen was required to "go back into his own Country" after the work was completed (41st), and the 42nd law required that White men who overstayed their welcome pay a fine of "one dollar for every day."

Arguably, the most fascinating aspects of these laws pertain to issues of race and gender. At the time these laws were drafted, some Mvskoke people owned slaves of African descent and practiced plantation-style agriculture, which was authorized by the national government. Several laws pertaining to slaves (sometimes called "Negroes") reflect a government in which slavery was an entrenched part of society. While individual owners were authorized to free their slaves under the 22nd law, other slave laws reflect the development of a clear racial hierarchy in which persons of African descent were afforded less protection from the Nation. Homicide against a "negro" for example, could be avenged by the mere payment of the "value" to his owner rather than execution (3rd). Mvskoke people who captured and returned "Runaway" slaves received compensation in the amount of fifteen dollars (26th). The 20th law is an antimiscegenation law, requiring the seizure of property from

Mvskoke people who married a "Negro," adding that "it is a disgrace to our Nation for our people to marry a Negro."

Even after removal to Indian Territory, chattel slavery remained a fairly common practice in the Creek Nation. Following the U.S. Civil War (in which many Mvskoke people aligned with the Confederacy), the Creek Nation signed a peace treaty in 1866, which, among other things, required that Creek people end the practice of slavery and bestow among former slaves "all the rights and privileges of native citizens, including an equal interest in the soil and national funds."[3] Despite this clear treaty language, the Creek Nation still struggles with the legacy of slavery in the twenty-first century. In 1979, when the Creek Nation ratified its current constitution, the citizenship provisions denaturalized the descendants of freedmen and -women by declaring that only persons who are "Muscogee (Creek) Indian by blood" would be eligible for citizenship.[4] Challenges to these constitutional provisions by descendants of freed people in the twenty-first century have thus far been rebuffed by MCN courts, including twice by the Supreme Court.

In terms of gender, four provisions are worthy of close examination. Two of these gendered laws provide for punishment of women for behavior that is not similarly circumscribed for men. The 46th law requires that a widow refrain from marrying again until permission is granted by her late husband's family. Failure to comply with the wishes of the family would result in corporal punishment and disfigurement. The same punishment could befall a woman who committed adultery (48th).

Conversely, two other laws reflect a society in which Mvskoke women were offered protection that may not have been granted to white women under American laws in the nineteenth century. The 19th law protects Mvskoke women and children from abandonment by white husbands, requiring that such a husband "leave all his property with his children for their support" when leaving the Nation. This law appears to be a newer version of a law found in the 1818 laws presented to Agent Mitchell. The 1818 law regarding abandonment by white men provides more substance in terms of legislative history, reading, "It has often happened that white men have come into our Nation poor, and taken an Indian woman to wife by which they had children, and when they have gotten their hands full, they have got tired of the country and left their wife & children to suffer, which we think very

Foreword xi

unjust." In American jurisprudence in the early nineteenth century, women were required to petition a court for property and alimony in the aftermath of divorce, and typically such awards were dependent on "fault," wherein the wife would have to prove extreme cruelty or abandonment to sustain a request for divorce and support. But the Creek law did not require the former wife of a white man to plead her case—the property was *required* to be left with the family regardless of the cause or circumstances of such abandonment.

Finally, the 35th law prohibiting rape offers another glimpse into a society that apparently did not always subscribe to patriarchal ideas. The penalty for those who "force woman and did it by force" was apparently left to the victim, providing agency for victims of sexual assault that did not exist in American law. The poignant phrase "what she say it be law"—the final phrase in the statute—stands in sharp contrast to Anglo-American principles in which sexual assault was closely intertwined with women's subservience to men. At no time has an American law ever provided victims of crimes with the agency to determine the appropriate punishment for a violent crime.

While there are many historical documents about the Mvskokvlke people prior to removal to Indian Territory, this particular document is one of only a few documents written by and for the people of the Creek Nation. It provides unique insight into how Mvskokvlke people governed themselves and ample material for contemporary researchers and scholars who are committed to the investigation and explication of tribal law in the United States.

SARAH DEER, J.D.

Notes

1. Jack B. Martin and Margaret McKane Mauldin, *A Dictionary of Creek/Muskogee* (Lincoln: University of Nebraska Press, 2000), xvii–xviii.

2. Sarah Deer and Cecilia Knapp, "Muscogee Constitutional Jurisprudence: Vhakv Em Pvtakv (the Carpet under the Law)," *Tulsa Law Review* 49 (2013): 125, 138.

3. Article 2, U.S. Treaty with the Creek Nation, June 14, 1866.

4. Muscogee (Creek) Nation Constitution, Article II, Sec. 1; Article III, Sec. 2 and 3 (1979).

Foreword

THIS slim volume containing the heretofore unpublished *Laws of the Creek Nation* is the first in a series of publications to be issued at irregular intervals by the University of Georgia Libraries. The series will be published under the imprint of the University of Georgia Press and will contain both source materials and reprints of rare items from the collections of the Libraries.

All titles will be available to other libraries on an exchange basis from the Gift and Exchange Section, Acquisitions Division, University of Georgia Libraries. To individuals and libraries or organizations which have no publications for exchange, they will be available by purchase from the University of Georgia Press.

The manuscript is a part of the Keith Read Collection of manuscripts which was donated to the Libraries in 1957 by the Wormsloe Foundation of Savannah.

                                    W. P. Kellam, Director
                                University of Georgia Libraries
December 1, 1959

Introduction

On January 7, 1825, Chilly McIntosh, son of the half-Scot Creek chief, General William McIntosh, wrote out for his cousin, Governor George M. Troup,[1] a copy of the laws of the Creek Nation. This was the second known attempt of the Creeks to collect their laws, an earlier version being committed to writing by General William McIntosh and other Creek leaders in 1818.[2] It seems that prior to 1818 all laws made in National Council were either kept by memory or in an unorganized manner in writing. After 1818 they were recorded as made or revised, and the original cumulative manuscript was in Chilly's care by virtue of his position as Clerk of the Creek National Council. At least he had been Clerk of Council until a few days previously when at Broken Arrow[3] he was "broke" for incompetence shortly before his father was "broke" as Speaker and fled for his life.

There had been stormy doings at Broken Arrow. The Creek National Council assembled there in December, 1824, as ordered by the United States commissioners,

---

[1] The two were first cousins. McIntosh's father, William, and Troup's mother, Katherine, were brother and sister, children of John McIntosh of McIntosh Bluff, Alabama.

[2] This earlier version, containing eleven laws and formulated at the request of D. B. Mitchell, Indian Agent, was published at a general meeting of the chiefs and warriors at Thleancotchean (Broken Arrow) on June 12, 1818. It was signed three days later by General William McIntosh and four other Creek leaders. All the earlier laws are included in the later compilation but with wide variation in some of the wording. The original manuscript of the 1818 laws is in the D. B. Mitchell Manuscript Collection, the Newberry Library, Chicago, Illinois.

[3] The seat of the Creek National Council, a Coweta town near Fort Mitchell on the west bank of the Chattahoochee River.

Duncan G. Campbell and David Meriwether, both Georgians with numerous local political affiliations. Their reason for calling the assembly was no secret. They had been duly commissioned to treat with the obvious purpose of securing for the State of Georgia the last of the Creek lands within the chartered limits of Georgia lying west of the Flint River.

A year previously the same two men had failed to gain from the Cherokees a cession of their lands, and negotiations had been continued in Washington between the Cherokee delegation, the Georgia delegation, and the Federal Government with no success whatsoever. Furthermore, the Creek chiefs back home had been kept quietly but fully informed from Washington by the Cherokee chief John Ross of the proceedings, by letters and by copies of all pertinent documents.

Frustrated in their Cherokee attempts, the Commissioners shifted their attack to the Creeks, from which quarter they had had some encouragement. When the delegations arrived at Broken Arrow on the first of December the atmosphere was ominous, explosive. In the intermittent December drizzle group after group of Indians arrived. Again and again extra rations were requested by the Commissioners until at length it was estimated that between six and ten thousand pairs of eyes were watching all that took place. They were apprehensive, distrustful eyes and they were all on William McIntosh.

The Indians' suspicion was not without foundation of fact. While it may be that McIntosh advocated a removal West partly because he realized the inevitability of white encroachment, it is equally true that avarice was his own particular one of the seven deadly sins. Although there can be no criticism of his conduct before 1817, the arrival of David Bridie Mitchell as Agent in that year altered things. Qualities which were hidden in McIntosh the brilliant warrior emerged in McIntosh the trader and

INTRODUCTION 3

tavern keeper, who at the same time was one of the five great chiefs in the Nation. Mitchell, whose motives in accepting the position as Agent were highly questionable,[4] soon found in McIntosh a willing pupil and able partner.

About the Agency, McIntosh was given a free hand in most matters, and in the distribution of the annuities there seem to have been numerous irregularities highly profitable both to Mitchell and McIntosh.[5] In fact, one suspects strongly that it was Mitchell who taught McIntosh his price. What stood worst against McIntosh at Broken

---

[4]Governor John Clark, a violent political enemy of Mitchell's, put the charge succinctly: "In November, 1815, General D. B. Mitchell was elected Governor of Georgia, for two years, and in the spring of 1817 he received the appointment of Agent of Indian Affairs, and for this office the government of Georgia was relinquished. As a man known to be ambitious of political distinction would not probably have made such a change with a view to public honor, it is natural to conclude that some pecuniary inducements must have led to it. And this is rendered more probable from the remark of the Agent himself, who was heard to remark that he had 'served the public long enough, and he would be d----d if he did not now serve himself!' " Clarke, John, *Considerations on the Purity of the Principles of William H. Crawford.* . . . Augusta: Printed at the *Georgia Advertiser* Office, 1819, p. 131. See also letter from Andrew Jackson to James Monroe, September 28, 1819 (in Jackson, Andrew, *Correspondence of Andrew Jackson,* edited by John Spencer Bassett. 7 volumes. Washington: Carnegie Institution, 1926-1935, pp. 433-37); and Mitchell, David Bridie, *An Exposition of the Case of the Africans, Taken to the Creek Agency, by Captain William Bowen, on Or About the 1st Dec'r. 1817.* Milledgeville: Camak & Hines, 1821.
[5]Little Prince to E. P. Gaines in Council at Broken Arrow, when asked what was the cause of the differences between McIntosh, the Agent, and John Crowell, answered, "All that he knows is that it was on account of Stinson, who was brought into the Nation, and who traded without a license; and because the Agent would not join with him in cheating the nation out of their annuity, which McIntosh and the former Agent, Mitchell, were in the habit of doing. McIntosh and Mitchell used to steal all our money, because they could write." U. S. Congress. House. Select Committee. *Report of the Select Committee of the House of Representatives, to which Were Referred the Messages of the President U. S. of the 5the and 8th February, And 2d March, 1827, with Accompanying Documents: And a Report And Resolutions of the Legislature of Georgia.* . . . 19th Congress, 2nd Session, House Report 98. Washington: Gales & Seaton, 1827, p. 449. For similar testimony see that of Joseph Hardage, pp. 421-22; William Hambly, p. 397; and Thomas Triplett, p. 390.

Arrow, however, was his conduct among the Cherokees during November of the preceding year.

McIntosh's complicity in the Creek cession of 1821 (he had been heavily bribed by the Georgians)[6] was not known to his people. Had it been he would probably have been executed at that time.[7] But what was known was his attempt to bribe the Cherokee chiefs to sell their lands the previous November (1823). The same Campbell and Meriwether had been treating with the Cherokees. McIntosh, present at the Council by virtue of his position as an honorary Cherokee chief,[8] approached John Ross and others with money, from an unknown source, and foolishly put his bribery attempt in writing. He was ignominiously exposed in open Council, broken as a Cherokee chief, and deported in complete disgrace. The original of the bribery letter, which still exists in the National Archives, was sent by Ross to Big Warrior along with a covering letter signed by Ross and a number of the most prominent Cherokees explaining the "painful and unpleasant" proceedings and concluding, "therefore, we advise you as brothers, to keep a strict watch over his conduct, or, if you do not, he will ruin your nation."[9]

---

[6] "Our prospects of obtaining land from the Indians upon our first arrival were gloomy, but they now begin to brighten. . . . General McIntosh is very unwell, but if his health should improve and the treaty be effected, he will pay you a visit in a few days for the purpose of obtaining money, and we are in hopes the fine opportunity of obtaining a vast acquisition of territory so highly beneficial to our State and fellow citizens generally, will not be neglected for the want of a little money, even if it should amount to forty thousand dollars." David Adams and Daniel Newnan to Governor John Clark, 31 December 1820. Unpublished letter, Governor John Clark File, Georgia State Department of Archives and History. It should also be remembered that this transaction set aside in addition for McIntosh's personal possession the valuable reserve at Indian Springs. For this holding, under the terms of the questionable treaty of Indian Springs (February, 1825) McIntosh was to receive an additional $25,000.

[7] U. S. Congress, House. Select Committee. *Op cit.*, pp. 322-23, 404.

[8] "An interchange of Chiefs has been established and continued from the time that there was but one Agent [Hawkins] for the four nations." *Ibid.*, p. 452n.

[9] *Ibid.*, p. 452.

INTRODUCTION

During the fall of 1824, before the meeting at Broken Arrow, far from taking measures to allay the apprehensions of the Creeks, the Commissioners only acted to aggravate them. Agents were sent into the Nation, notably William W. Williamson (Campbell's nephew) and Joel Bailey (McIntosh's business partner and tavern keeper at Indian Springs). These Agents systematically attempted to bribe every one of the older Indian countrymen who had the greatest influence with the natives to use all their influence to promote the treaty. Notable among these were Nimrod Doyell (Hawkins' old assistant) and William Hambly, the Nation's chief interpreter.[10]

Such an approach could not possibly have been more inept in a country where space seemed only to magnify each whisper into a shout. Bailey forgot himself so far as to try both bribery and threats simultaneously, even on Little Prince, but the old man confronted him stonily with such a contemptuous and ominous silence that, on the good advice of his interpreter, Bailey retreated forthwith.[11]

During the summer of 1824 an old and very strong law was re-proclaimed: Anyone, "however great he might be, even Big Warrior, Little Prince, or McIntosh,"[12] should he sell another foot of land to the Georgians would be put to death. This law was first made when the Chiefs met their new Agent, Mitchell, on the west bank of the Ocmulgee in July, 1817. At that time they consented to a small cession of land (consummated 22 January 1818) but simultaneously enacted the above law. It was said later that McIntosh himself proposed it.

This law was repeated again with dire mentions of "gun and rope" at Pole Cat Springs, and a copy of the "talk" was published in a Montgomery, Alabama, paper in early November, 1824. A copy of this paper was handed

---
[10]*Ibid.*, p. 419.
[11]*Ibid.*, pp. 420-21.
[12]*Ibid.*, pp. 455-57.

to the Commissioners at the Flint River on their way to Broken Arrow. Consequently they were fully aware, as was McIntosh, of the dangerous position in which he was being placed.

Negotiations did not actually begin at Broken Arrow until December the fourth. After the Commissioners presented their credentials in the council square, McIntosh, with characteristic boldness, made the first move. The Cherokees, he said, had accused him of offering land to the whites. The charge was false and made solely to discredit him in the eyes of his own people. He then turned to Campbell and asked him to state to the Council whether or not his statement was true. "Col. Campbell then rose, and stated it [the charge] to be false, and gave his honor to the Council, for the truth of the assertion."[13] This interesting performance, a sad reflection on the integrity of both actors,[14] was partially convincing. It and McIntosh's vigorous and eloquent talk against any cession of land[15] resulted in a rather reluctant decision of the Chiefs to make McIntosh Speaker for the Nation in these talks.

The Indian position was firmly against cession. As days of drizzling rain passed by, suspicions and tensions mounted. Strict laws were made in Council against any secret talks with the Commissioners. On the third day Josiah Gray, a half-breed chief, was caught in secret conference with the Commissioners and ordered by Little Prince "to take the track back home," and, if he did not obey within four hours "they would think further about."[16]

On the other hand, the Commissioners were also distrustful. The Agent John Crowell was kept under close watch. In fact Campbell roomed with him. The chief

---
[13]*Ibid.*, p. 395.
[14]*Ibid.*, p. 814.
[15]*Ibid.*, p. 389.
[16]*Ibid.*, p. 690.

interpreter, Hambly, was kept under similar close scrutiny because the Commissioners had good reason to think that neither he nor Crowell had his whole heart squarely behind the treaty. Crowell certainly did not. He was in that rare and enviable position in Georgia politics where his stand not only served his self interests but was also patently the proper and just position. The Commissioners watched Crowell and Hambly. The Indians watched McIntosh—and were not long in catching him.

The Commissioners must have been under the delusion that they were invisible. At any rate, they behaved with such naivete in an explosive situation that some such conclusion seems justified. Chilly ran a tavern near Broken Arrow. McIntosh, of course, stayed there. It soon became apparent that Campbell was making frequent trips to the tavern. Campbell's nephew, William W. Williamson, was also staying at the tavern and his chief business seems to have been arranging clandestine meetings between McIntosh and the Commissioners. They would meet at night at an appointed place where "the Commissioners, with McIntosh seated between them on a log, would give him his cue what to say in Council the next day; and often remained there till near break of day in the morning."[17] Naturally they were observed and the visits were reported in Council. On December the thirteenth, McIntosh was broken as Speaker.

McIntosh was furious at this disgrace. That night he had a tense conversation with Nimrod Doyell in Doyell's quarters. He vowed that he would sell the lands despite the Chiefs. Doyell said that much distress would result. "McIntosh replied he did not care; that three thousand dollars in the pockets of his friends, would take them any where. McIntosh also asked witness if he had any

---

[17]*Ibid.*, p. 447.

powder, and upon being answered in the affirmative, he said: Well, keep your gun in order and when you hear a *fuss*, come to my house."[18]

About the same time that night McIntosh's daughter, who was staying as a student in the house of the Reverend Isaac Smith, burst into the house exclaiming that a party of warriors was on the way to kill her father. But no "fuss" developed. McIntosh slipped from a window and made his escape into the night.

McIntosh retreated to the upper ferry at Coweta, where he had adherents. The Commissioners, completely abandoning decorum, left the Council sitting at Broken Arrow and galloped off after him. They found McIntosh, and though he was willing to sign a treaty by himself, the Commissioners' instructions expressly forbade such a unilateral transaction. Their only recourse was to fume, plan for a future meeting at a place farther from the heart of the Nation, and hope for obtaining altered instructions from Washington.

The thwarted Commissioners straggled back to Broken Arrow breathing threats and recriminations. The disappointed Campbell did not even return to the Council, but Meriwether did. Doyell testified that "in the verbal talks of the Commissioners, they threatened the council that, if they did not comply with their demands, the Georgia people would extend their laws over the nation."[19]

The meeting broke up with the Indians not budging an inch from their position and the frustrated and furious Commissioners attempting to fix the blame for their failure first on Crowell, who had maintained an attitude of "strict neutrality," and then on the sub-agent, Walker, who was a son-in-law of Big Warrior, and who had written the Tuckabatchee and Pole Cat Springs declara-

---

[18] *Ibid.*, p. 418.
[19] *Ibid.*, p. 419.

INTRODUCTION 9

tions. Most of the Cherokee correspondence was rounded up (notably missing were McIntosh's bribery letter and the letter of the Cherokee chief that accompanied it), and the Commissioners repaired to Milledgeville. Campbell almost immediately set out for Washington.

McIntosh, Chilly, and a handful of the "friendly chiefs" found the Nation currently too warm for them and also headed for Milledgeville. Here McIntosh proposed that he and his party should go to Washington themselves, but Troup prevented them, insisting that Campbell would obtain the desired concessions from the government.

The subject of "the law" and McIntosh's danger were discussed at length. McIntosh's position with his white friends and his near kinsman, Governor Troup, was that the talks at Tuckabatchee and Pole Cat Springs were not laws at all, and he feared no trial under them. However, he said " . . . there are some who would be glad for a pretext to have me murdered; many of the Upper Town chiefs are hostile to me, and many are still living who I helped to chastise, and whose relations I had to kill, in the late war, as enemies of the whites. . . ."[20] This statement was only about half true. There was no doubt in the minds of Little Prince, Big Warrior, and Opothlo Yohole as to the validity of the law. They were the leaders in the decision to execute McIntosh, and all three were leaders of the friendly Indian faction in the Creek War.

Chilly had brought along with him to Milledgeville many of the public papers of the National Council, including the official list of laws. William Lott later remarked, after testifying to the existence of the death law, "There are many penal laws in the nation that are

---

[20] *Ibid.*, p. 814.

not in writing. The few written laws that there are, witness has understood Chilly has run away with."[21]

Apparently, at the meeting in Milledgeville of those Indians and Georgians who were interested in the sale of Indian lands, the death law was prominent in discussion. Governor Troup must have requested from Chilly a copy of the laws, and that copy is the one being considered here. It is in Chilly's handwriting and signed by him. At the end of the document is the inscription, "It is understood that these are the laws at present in force in the Creek Nation and that none other are of any authority." This inscription, though unsigned, is in the handwriting of Governor Troup.[22]

McIntosh's end is all too well known. The following month (February) a palpably fraudulent treaty was concluded at Indian Springs between the Commissioners and a small group of Indians, most of whom were unqualified to act for the Nations. It was one of the first documents to cross the desk of the newly-elected and politically-harassed John Quincy Adams. In spite of a letter written by the Agent Crowell, accompanying the treaty warning that it was invalid, it was signed and ratified. As a direct result, there was a turbulent meeting of the Creek Council at Broken Arrow in late April and an execution party was secretly named. In the early hours of May 1st, the party surrounded McIntosh's home and put fire to it, permitting the escape of women, children, and whites. McIntosh defended himself valiantly, but at last presented himself in the doorway. He fell in a hail of bullets, was dragged into the yard, and there in the glare of his burning home was knifed to death. "He died by his own mouth," was the way the Indians put it.

---

[21] *Ibid.*, p. 432.
[22] A positive identification of this as Governor Troup's handwriting was made by O. B. Bell, handwriting expert for the Liberty National Bank, Savannah, Georgia.

INTRODUCTION

Although the list of laws was frequently referred to by Governor Troup and the Commissioners as they inveighed against the "illegality" of McIntosh's "murder," the document was never produced. This fact is remarkable since literally hundreds of documents, many trivial, bearing on the Indian Springs treaty, McIntosh's death, and the culpability of the Agent Crowell appeared in all manner of newspapers and were eventually gathered and printed in a single body in the voluminous (846 pages of small print) *House Report No. 98*.

The reason for the non-appearance of the document is evident. Although the famous "Death Law" was not on the list, another, "Law 33th," was in itself an adequate instrument to accomplish McIntosh's execution. Law 33 stated: "And be it farther enacted if any person or persons should tell such lies as should brought to disturpence of the Nation the punish shall be death." The "Death Law" of 1817 itself was sufficiently specific and well understood so that the Creek Council never even bothered to point to this weaker law.

Despite Troup's unsigned subscription that he understood these to be all the laws in force in the Creek Nation and "that none other are of any authority" it is perfectly obvious that this document was no attempt to unify and systematize Creek law. One has the impression that these laws were made in Council, one by one, haphazardly, as individual situations arose. They are laws made in a changing culture, calculated to deal with problems beyond the scope of ancient Creek custom, problems arising out of contact with the white man—cattle raising, slave owning, the use of United States currency, systematic agriculture, trading, and the presence of a stream of passing settlers on the way across the Nation to the Alabama and Mississippi territories. Then there were problems of inheritance which derived out of all these factors.

Significantly some of these laws are dated 1817, the year after the death of Agent Benjamin Hawkins. It is very likely that this is the year in which the law list was initiated. Hawkins had been devoted to his redskin charges and had done much to preserve them as a nation after the Creek War. When he first went into Creek country his journal amply reveals the sorry and demoralized state of affairs he found. When he left, despite the Creek War (which was essentially part of the War of 1812), he had done much to better the Creeks individually and to strengthen them as a nation by adapting their ancient form of government into a more effective centralized form.

When Hawkins first became familiar with Creek customs, he was particularly offended by the strict observance of the old law, a life for a life, no matter how accidental a death might have been, and under which a perfectly innocent person could suffer. He never tired of citing irrational instances of this bloody custom in his journal and during his agency did much to mollify the hard, old way. The fact that the first seven of these laws are laws easing the old custom is probably a tribute to Hawkins. The Creeks relied greatly on Hawkins' judgment in these matters, and it seems likely that they felt no need to record such laws until after his death.

In format the Laws consist of four folded sheets (16 pages) of unlined and unwatermarked paper, with a fifth sheet of the same paper being used for a cover. The dimensions are 12⅜ x 7 13/16 inches, and creases show that the document was formerly folded twice to a 4 x 7 13/16 size. Round holes and slits in the left margin indicate that it was both sewed with cord and tied together with a ribbon at some time in its history. Nine pages are covered with writing in legible script, with scant margins on all four sides. The front edges are slightly frayed and the inner margin shows a little damage caused by the slits cut for the ribbon. The black ink originally used has faded to a dark brown. Except for these slight imperfections the manuscript is in good condition.

The document is in Chilly McIntosh's hand and signed by him on the forepage. The slips of Chilly's pen have a certain quaint charm to them. One can fairly hear the thick Creek accent in such mistakes as "big" for "pig," "tudy" for "duty," "soper" for "sober," and "indefare" for "interfere." He wrote in a good, firm, graceful hand. Later his English became practically faultless.

Chilly died many years later after the Creek removal to Oklahoma, a valued and effective member of his faction among the Creeks.

Savannah, Georgia   Antonio J. Waring

Laws of Muscogee Nation

Law 1st Murder shall be punished with death the person who commits the act shall be only one punished and only upon good proof 1817

Law 2nd If a man kill another person and it can be proved to have done by accident he shall not be punished —

Law 3rd If a negro kill an Indian the negro shall suffer death, and if an Indian kill a negro he shall pay the owner the value. If person not able to pay the value shall suffer death —

Law 4th If a man horse kills another person he shall be said nothing to the owner about it, and if two persons ride one horse together and the horse flings them, and one is killed and the other lives to get up shall be considered an accident

Law 5th If a man take a weapon in hand and goes to kill another person and the another goes to kill happens to kill first, and the fact be so proved he shall be forgiven as he killed the man to save his own life

Law 6th If a man should killed another in a town drinking, and it can be proved to the satisfaction of the chief, that when he committed the act that he is as out of senses, and that he and all his people were friendly to the person killed previous to his death, there he shall not be punished but forgiven —

Law 7th If a man fired his gun at Deer Bird or any thing else. and he should be so unfortunate as to wound or kill another person it shall be considered an accident and of course must not be punished

FIRST PAGE OF THE LAWS

of the Creek Nation Should take up white man with family into his house under employ for any business, and if the chiefs Should Complain to the employer to have them ordered out of the Nation before done. if they Should Steal; the person who Keeps them Shall pay the full value of the losses

Law 56th If a white man Should want to keep store or stand in the Nation he shall come before the national chiefs and Warriers and is Willing to pay what Sum the national Chiefs and Warriers may ask and there he Shall obtain license from the Agent of the Nation

Laws Ended this day 15th March 1824th A.D.

It is understood that these are the laws at present in force in the Creek Nation & that none other are of any authority here

Laws of the Creek Nation

Laws of the Muscogee Nation

Law 1st Murder shall be punished with death the person who commits the act shall be the only one punish and only upon good proofs (1817)[1]

Law 2nd If a man Kill another person and it can be provened to have done by accident he shall not be punished —

Law 3th If a negro Kill an Indian the negro shall ~~be~~ suffer death. and if an Indian Kill a negro

---

[1] The first seven laws, as well as several others, modify the old custom by which a life was taken for a life regardless of the circumstances under which the victim lost his. Hawkins records an incident when one boy who accidentally shot another in a hunting accident would have been killed and buried in the same grave except for the intervention of a single old Chief. This principle was even carried so far that if a horse tied at a trading post should kill a man, the responsibility for the death was fixed on the owner of the house, the owner of the horse, or the man who tied the beast there. We see in "Law 4th" provisions for precisely this sort of situation. For a general discussion, see Swanton, John Reed, *Social Organization and Social Usages of the Indians of the Creek Confederacy*. (In U. S. Bureau of Ethnology, Forty-second Annual Report . . . 1924-25. Washington: Government Printing Office, 1928), pp. 338-44.

This first law refers specifically to the custom whereby, if the killer himself could not be apprehended, a clan member could be put to death in his stead, and the offended clan would be completely satisfied. For example, in 1802 the Indian murderer of a white man named Moreland escaped. The Indians produced in his place a kinsman, "a bad man," who had helped him escape, and who, they said, could be executed on the spot if it pleased Hawkins. However, apprehensive of Hawkins' strong feelings on guilt and innocence, they had an alternative suggestion: that they turn the man over to Hawkins to be kept closely confined. In the meanwhile, "if Colonel Hawkins will permit them to report that he is executed, . . . the murderer will return and they will put him to death." Hawkins would have none of this. Hawkins, Benjamin, *Letters of Benjamin Hawkins, 1796-1806*. (Collections of the Georgia Historical Society, v. 9.) Savannah: Georgia Historical Society, 1916, p. 424.

he shall pay the owner the value. If person not able to pay the value shall suffer death —

Law 4th   If a man horse Kills another person he shall be said nothing to the owner about it, and if two person ride one horse together and the horse flings them, and one is Killed and the [other] lives to get up shall be considered an accident.

Law 5th   If a man take a weapon in hand and goes to Kill another person and the man he goes to Kill happens to Kill first, and the fact be so proven he shall be forgiven as he Killed the man to save his own life

Law 6th   If a man should Killed another in a rum drinking and it can be proven to the satisfaction of the Chiefs that when he committed the act that he was out of senses, and that he and all his people were friendly to the person Killed previous to his death, then he shall not be punished but forgiven —

Laws 7th If a man fired his gun at Deer, Bird or any thing else, and he should be so unfortunate as to wound or Kill another person it shall be considered an accident and of course must not be punished

Laws 8th Stealing shall be punished as follows for the first offence the thief shall be whiped for the second offence shall be croped. for the third offence he shall be put to death =

Law 9th   If a man stolen another he shall pay forty Dollars and in case he has no property to pay the fine he shall be punished the same as stealing the law for stealing Viz . . . first time whiped 2d Croped 3d put to death =

Law 10th If any person give faulse evidence by which

another suffers punishment he shall receive the same punishment, which he inflicted upon the one against whom he stated the faulshood =

Law 11th   When a [man] dies and has children [they] shall have the property [and] his other relations shall not take the property to the injury of His children —

Law 12th   Should any of the friendly Indians owe a debt to Hostile, Indians owe a debt to friendly Indians may have been contracked (1817) before this time neither of them, shall to the other =²

Law 14th [sic]   Friendly Indians must pay all debt due to each other =

Law 14th   Should two persons swap horse the bargain shall be considered good unless one of the party proves that he was drunk at the time he swaped, and in case he makes these fact Know in five days after the swap his horse shall be returned to him, but if he does not cl[aim] within five days the bargain shall be considered good, and cannot get his horse back =

Law 15th   No person shall received for damages done to his Crope by an other the stock of an other person unless he has a lawfull fence around his field and in case he should have a lawfull fence, and the stock of another person should injured his property in that case he shall recover for all damages, but if he has not a lawfull fence, and he should kill the stock of another person

---

²"Friendly" and "hostile" Indians in this sense refer to the sides taken in the recent Creek War, which was essentially an extension of the War of 1812. The Hostiles were still very much on probation.

LAWS OF THE CREEK NATION

for injuring his property he shall pay for all he Kill =

Law 16th Should any person set fire to the woods where he know, that there was Sows or Big [pig] or Calfs and any of them should be injured thereby he shall pay all damages to the owner, but if he can proove that he did not know, of such stock being there he shall not pay damages =

Law 17th If [a man] goes out a fire hunting and should kill property belonging to another person, and he can proove it was done accidently he shall not pay, if it can be prooven, that he did it intentionally he shall pay the owner =[3]

Law 18th If a man has a dog and the dog should run away and Kill property belonging to another person the owner, shall not pay but if it can be prooven that the dog owner set the dog on in the case he shall pay =

Law 19th Should a White man take an Indian woman as a wife and have children by her and he goes out of the Nation he shall leave all his property with his children for their support =[4]

Law 20th If any of our people have children and Negroes and either of the children should take a Negro for as a husband or wife — and should Said child have a property given to it by his or her

---

[3] Fire hunting is the practice of hunting at night by lantern or torch. Deer seem to be fascinated by the light, are easily approached, and their shiny eyes make a perfect target. Needless to say, in the darkness, horses and cows were not infrequent victims.

[4] The trader and the Indian countryman often abandoned their Indian families and returned to the settlements. McIntosh's own father, William McIntosh of Mallow, did so. He left his two Indian wives and children and eventually returned to the Georgia coast. There he married his cousin, Barbara, produced a family, and finally died respectably.

parent the property shall be taken from them and divide among the rest of the children as it is a disgrace to our ~~people~~ Nation for our people to marry a Negro[5]

Law 21st Slave shall not raise property of any kind. . If the master does not take it from them the law makers shall and they may do as they please with the property —

Law 22nd If any ~~person~~ man should think proper to Sett his Negroe free he shall be considered a freeman by the Nation —

Law 23th Prisoners taken in War shall not be Considered or traded as slave and it shall be the tudy [duty] of the law makers to make them as free of ourselfs[6]

Law 24th If any Stud Horse or Bull Should Kill any man, Horse or Cows the master of the Stud Horse or Bull Shall not pay damages to the owner of the property Killed or injured —

Law 25th If any person not living in the Nation buy a Horse from an Indian without a permit from the agent Big Warrior or Little Prince and Should lose the said Horse we will not aid or assist him in finding the Horse, but if he has a permit from either of the above named persons we will help him to get his horse —

Law 26th There [are] four persons appointed to receive runaway Negroes and astray Horses, any per-

---

[5] This law and several others reflect the problem created by the presence of Negroes in the Creek Nation. They fell into three groups: slaves, freedmen, and runaways.

[6] Most of the worst of the early friction between the Creeks and Carolinians resulted from raiding for Indian slaves and the resulting trade. It was one of the main causes of the Yemassee War of 1715. It is interesting to note that even at this late date a specific stipulation had to be made against it.

LAWS OF THE CREEK NATION

sons carrying them to the above mention, shall be paid as follow Runaway Negroes fifteen Dollars, the owner must pay the Nation fifty Dollars Astray Horse two Dollars the owner must pay the Nation five Dollars[7]

Law 27th   If an Indian lose any part of his Clothing, and they Should be found by another and the finder does not tell of his having them he shall be punish=

Law 28th   If any one or two Towns belonging to our Nation remove from the Nation to any other Country they shall have no claims upon this Country without the Consent of the Hole Nation (1819)[8]

Law 29th   If a man has a wife and he Should make use of or unfortunately lose his propperty of any discription and they Should part, the husband cannot call upon the woman for pay —

Law 30th   If a man makes a field and in doing so he turns a road belonging to the Nation he Shall not be interrupted, and if any wishes to erect a mill he is at liberty to do so=[9]

---

[7]Control of horse stealing and runaway Negroes was one of the major vexations of the Agent. When Hawkins first took the Agency he found a thriving traffic in stolen horses across the Nation, the chief market being in Florida.
[8]This law, which McIntosh well knew, is precisely the one he was trying to evade in making a separate treaty with the Georgians.
[9]This law would seem to reflect a somewhat more definite individual apportionment of agricultural land among the Creeks than has been assumed in the past. Since all land was National property, one assumes that this law provided for the individual who plowed beyond his personal allotment. As for the provision regarding the right of an individual to erect a mill, control of streams seems to have been vested in the local town, and bridges and ferries belonged to the individual town and were maintained by it (See Crowell to Gaines, 3 Oct. 1825., H. R. #98, p. 574). One supposes that this section of the law provided that some leeway be given to the individual Indian in the control of streams.

LAWS OF THE CREEK NATION 23

Law 31st   No Master Shall be bound for any trade or bargain made by his slave

Law 32nd   No person belonging to the Creek Nation shall go into any of the United States Territories or Cherokee Nation and procure goods or any thing else upon a Credit, And should any citizens of the United States, Territories or Cherokee Nation sells goods on a Credit to any person residing in the Nation they do it upon their own responsibility, as the Chief and Warriors, will not indefare between the parties, when any Claims is brought before them

Law 32nd [sic]   If the men who are or shall be appointed to put the laws in force shall neglect their tudy [sic] or abuse their power by doing injustice to any one under color of their authority they shall make satisfaction to the party injured, and be broke, and any one Hinden them for doing, their tudy or offers to commit violence upon their persons the party offending him shall be punished at the discretion of the Chiefs of the town they may belong to[10]

Law 33th   And it be farther enacted if any person or persons Should tell such lies as should brought to disturpence of the Nation the punish shall be death

Law 34th   And be it farther enacted if any slave should Kill a slave such punishment shall be death=

---

[10] These enforcement officers, variously called "'lawyers," "lawmenders" or the "light horse," were a post-Hawkins institution. A law violated was regarded as physically broken and the "law-makers" remade the law by punishing the offender. They were given the rank of lesser chiefs, and it was from this essentially new social group that McIntosh recruited most of his signers to the treaty of February, 1825. (See also "Law 47th" and "54th.")

Law 35th And be it farther enacted if any person or persons should under take to force woman and did it by force, it shall be left to the woman what punishment she Should satisfied with to whip or pay what she say it be law=

Law 36th And be it farther enacted if any person or persons borrow a horse and the horse Should die before Return to the owner, and if the owner of the ~~owner~~ horse Should mention before lone [loan] if the horse should Should die in his hand before return that he should pay full price and if never mention before lone it shall be his own loss

Law 37th And be it farther enacted if a woman should Kill a child and proof on her that she was gilty of it first whip second crop a third death=[11]

Law 38 And be it farther enacted if two persons Should steal and one Should tell on the other one should be whiped and the teller stand Clair=

Law 39th And be it farther enacted, if a man and wife should steal, while living together and after parted one Should tell on the other both Shall be punish as a thief.

Law 40th And be it farther enacted if any person or persons should die without leaving property behind or haden [had not any] the Creditator shall loss. if he had property when they died, and put it into some persons hand the creditator shall look unto him for Payment.

Law 41st And be it farther enacted if any person or persons should employed a White Man to

---

[11]Infanticide was a maternal privilege and was apparently quite common. See Swan and Milfort as quoted in Swanton, *op. cit.*, p. 345.

LAWS OF THE CREEK NATION 25

work, after work done he shall go back into his own Country, shall not stay no longer than the work done=

Law 42nd If a White Man should be ordered out of the Nation and if he should stay longer than the time expired he shall pay one dollar for every day=

Law 43th If a person or persons should give bad talk ~~to the~~ against Warriors or chiefs, he shall be punish by the Section 8th

Law 44th The Citizens of the Nation shall pay Taxes for every year, or twelve months twenty five cts per head ten dollars stand stores and Ferriage.

Law 45th If any person or persons should blow for rain or poisen they shall not be interrupted[12]

Law 46th Man and Wife if a husband Should die, it Shall be left to the kin people [of the man] who died how long she should be a widow ~~for four~~ two three or for [sic] years ~~and before four year ends~~ and if she should be widow for four years and before four years end, if she Should get to a man and proof on her She Shall be Whip and Cut the ears & Set her free.[13]

---

[12] This law refers to the ceremony of the Creek medicine man to make rain or blow it away. He would stick the handle of an ax in the ground with the blade pointing to the cloud, sing his song or chant four times, and blow toward the cloud. His blowing was supposed to cause the cloud to separate and pass over. To make rain he would find a spring of water and chant his song for rain. The word *poisen* is probably an English version of the Creek word *pof'ketv*, to blow. (Information furnished by Miss Theda Wammack, Curator, The Creek Memorial Association, Okmulgee, Oklahoma.)

[13] E. A. Hitchcock wrote, "An attempt was made in 1840 to abolish a custom giving to the relations of a husband on his death the power of keeping a widow secluded and forbidding her second marriage for a period of four years. They attempted to restrict the period to 12 months, but the people would not listen to it and the council yielded to the public voice and repealed the law in 1841." Hitchcock, Ms. notes. Quoted in Swanton, *op. cit.*, p. 334.

LAWS OF THE CREEK NATION

Law 47th   If a lawyer Should violate the law first and Second shall be tole and the third time shall be broke as a chief —

Law 48th   If a man may, have a wife and lived with her and his wife should sleep with another man and husband proof on her he Shall cut Whip his wife and the man Cut the ears off. And Set her free=

Law 49th   No person shall permit a White into the Nation to live except the hole Nation agree to it=

Law 50th   If any person or persons Should get Kill in playing ball Shall not be punish if person Should take Stick and Knock person and Kill it Shall be death —

Law 51st   Person or persons Should take man wife way and be punish for it and Should die with it the punisher Shall be Kill as a murder=

Law 52th   If one family Should Kill Brother or Sister the punishment Shall be death by Section 1st

Law 53th   If person Should get drunk and want to fight it Shall be Rope untill he get Soper=

Law 54th   And be farther enacted if person or persons Should violate the law of the Creek Nation shall be punished by the law of Section 8th And their Shall be one person appointed to command the lite horse, to punish the violator, and he who appoint it, to Command, he Shall See justice done. And and not take property, but be punish by law

Law 55th   And be it farther enacted if person or persons of the Creek Nation Should take up White Man with family into his house under employ for or any business and if the chiefs Should Complain to the employer to have them order out of the Nation before done. if they Should Steal, the person who Keep them Shall pay the full value of the losses

Law 56th If a White man Should want to keep store or stand in the Nation he shall come before the National Chiefs and Warriors and is Willing to pay what Sum the National Chiefs and Warriors may ask and than he shall obtain license from the Agent of the Nation.

Laws Ended this day 15th
March 1824th A.D.

It is understood that these are the laws at present in force in the Creek Nation & that none other are of any authority there.[14]

---

[14]These final lines are in the handwriting of Governor George M. Troup.